KU-560-637

Sir Alexander Fleming
Man of Penicillin

First Published in 1981
by Alloway Publishing Ltd.,
High Street, Ayr.

Printed in Scotland.
by Walker & Connell Ltd.,
Hastings Square, Darvel,
Ayrshire.

ISBN 0 907526 06 3

Sir Alexander Fleming
Man of Penicillin

JOHN MALKIN

ALLOWAY PUBLISHING, AYR.

Sir Alexander Fleming

F.R.S., M.B., B.Sc., F.R.C.S., F.R.C.P.

COMMANDER OF THE LEGION OF HONOUR

FOREWORD

by Lady Amalia Fleming

This book has given me great pleasure. It is an excellent account of my husband's life. As a doctor myself deeply involved in his work I am particularly impressed by its scientific accuracy — something quite unusual for an author not himself medically qualified.

My husband was a quiet man. If he had any fault it was that he took his virtues to extremes. He was shy of competition with others and of any self-promotion. Nevertheless I am sure he would have enjoyed this small book.

Its publication in his native Ayrshire is especially fitting; he always looked upon his early days in Scotland with great affection and pride and retained his Scottish character throughout his life.

Amalia Fleming

Athens,
Greece.

June, 1981

CONTENTS

ALEXANDER FLEMING

MAN OF PENICILLIN

No compelling urge, or desire, attracted Alexander Fleming to medicine. When he decided at the age of twenty to enter upon a career in the profession, it was not the result of some deep, spiritual conviction that he had been called to allay suffering in the human race.

Alexander Fleming, the farmer's son from Darvel in Ayrshire, destined to make one of the greatest discoveries in chemotherapy in the history of medicine, changed from the role of clerk to the role of doctor for no more reason than that a brother, himself a doctor, had concluded that a medical role would offer him a better chance to develop the many outstanding natural gifts with which he had been endowed.

Having made this change of course, however, Fleming had no difficulty pursuing his work with Hippocratic dedication. Never once from then on did he set limit of time or physical strength upon himself. He filled his medical role completely, giving to it unselfishly of mind and body and showing a personal and passionate involvement with the sick.

It was at Lochfield, an upland farm of 800 acres four miles north of Darvel, that Alexander Fleming was born on 6 August, 1881. Leased by his father, Hugh, from the Earl of Loudoun, Lochfield marched with land in Lanark and Renfrew. To the north lay Overmoor, farmed by the Loudons, life-long friends of the Flemings. Boundary in the north-east was a bog with the picturesque name of The Gull Haggs. A dry stane dyke marked both the eastern boundary of Lochfield and the boundary between Ayrshire and Lanarkshire. Glen Water and Loch Burn flowed together to form the boundary to the south-east.

Front view of Lochfield.

Lochfield as it is today.

Set in moorland, the nearest house at least a mile distant, Lochfield existed in isolation. It was intimidating country, as capable of breaking a man as bending a tree, and yet there was in its ever-present hostility and oft-recurring fury the sinister power to lure and cajole the settler into a trial of strength. The earth around Lochfield did not readily yield a living, but demanded of farming communities hard and constant toil, ungrudging co-operation one with the other, and a close sympathetic affinity with soil and beast. The Flemings survived the shock of this conflict with Nature and emerged as hardier, more resistant stock.

Twice married, Hugh Fleming had a family of four by each wife. Jane, Hugh, Tom and Mary were born of his first wife. He was sixty years old when he married again, this time Grace Morton, from Bransfield Farm. By her, he had a third daughter, Gracie, and another three sons – John, Alexander (the discoverer of penicillin) and Robert.

Grace Morton was a woman of strong maternal instinct and generous nature. She was the first of five women, three of them outstanding in their own right, who were to help significantly towards the fashioning of Alexander Fleming for the great part which Destiny was to call upon him to play.

Taking over a family of four when she became Hugh Fleming's second wife, Grace Fleming gathered them as closely and tenderly to herself as she did her own children. Having accepted Hugh Fleming as her husband, no doubt she would feel a moral and legal obligation to mother the family by his first wife. But obligation is not enough in such a delicate human relationship. Grace Fleming was not moved by mere obligation but by qualities of love and compassion, and these were the qualities which allowed her to make of her two families, one family, each of its eight members a brother or sister to all the others, bound together in companionship as long as they lived, respecting and working for one another.

Grace Fleming's main contribution to her eight children was

to give them a protective love and understanding. Given this great maternal legacy, this strengthening security, the Fleming children each developed an unshakable independence of mind and action, and an unquestioning loyalty to each other.

All the Flemings made their way comfortably through the world. No doubt, the great natural talents they possessed would have been sufficient on their own to see them safely and happily to journey's end. But, there is equally no doubt that it was their mother, Grace Morton Fleming, who endowed them with the supreme confidence and dogged resolve they showed, the boys especially, when they moved away from the safety of Lochfield and into a bigger and less certain world. What else could have allowed Alec, at the age of thirteen, and Robert, even younger, to make their way to London, secure a place for themselves, and settle to a life which was the antithesis of Lochfield.

The mother of the Fleming children was a unique person. When her husband died, she managed Lochfield along with her elder son, Hugh. And when he married, she graciously gave way to the new mistress of Lochfield, Kate Loudon of Overmoor, moved to London, and resumed her motherly care of Tom, John, Alec and Robert. Her influence upon the family was always benign.

When she died in 1927, Alec, her favourite son, so it is said, had married a woman who was to continue the uncomplaining self-sacrificing role so effectively played by the older woman.

Lochfield was the making of the Fleming children. To the boys, it was an adventure playground on a grand scale, their own private country park. Because Hugh and Tom were much older, John, Alec and Robert tended to get together to explore the delightful world of Lochfield. They had no money to spend, but this was no obstacle to enjoyment. Barefoot in summer they roamed over field and moor, keeping company with a great variety of bird life — grouse, partridge, golden plover, peewit, whaup, skylark, mosscheeper, snipe, wild duck, hawk, sand-piper, ring-ouzel, heron, sand martin and corncrake. Sometimes, they would gather a few peewit eggs, and sell them to local grocers at 4d each for shipment to London where they were considered a delicacy of haute cuisine.

The upper reaches of Glen Water and Fleming's grandson Michael.

Glen Water, Burn Loch, and the Pogiven provided trout for rod and line or the lesser sport of guddling. The rocky flanks of the rivers were scaled by the boys to get at the blackberries which grew there in luxuriant abundance. Here, in the pools, the boys learned to swim and dive. With the help of an old pet dog, they trapped rabbits which had run to cover in holes in the embankment. Alec's arm in one end, Robert's or John's in the other — and the prize to whoever caught the poor fugitive by its hind legs.

Close and sympathetic awareness of the natural world of Lochfield bred a keen power of observation and a disciplined patience in the Fleming boys — qualities which were to be applied by Alec with spectacular success in his work as a research scientist.

When the weather was poor, Fleming restlessness had still to be satisfied. Confined to living quarters, Alec tended to occupy himself mainly with reading or some creative, manual exercise. Near the Loch Burn, there was a bed of clay which could be used for modelling. This was fashioned by the Fleming boys into shapes of varying kinds, mounted on stones in the burn to be eventually washed away. Sometimes, the clay was taken back home, and the work of modelling was continued in an outhouse. Time was always constructively occupied at Lochfield.

Though not old enough to need to take part in the day-to-day duties of the farm, John, Alec and Robert were usually involved in one way or another. Neighbours came along to help with the sheep-clipping, and the boys made a useful contribution by bringing the sheep from the pens to the shearers.

Harvesting the oat crop and bringing in the hay saw every manjack fully occupied for days on end. This was the time of year when itinerant Irish labourers were taken on so that the harvest could be secured before the rains came.

Winters were severe at Lochfield. Blown in by gales from the Atlantic, snow covered the land deeply for miles around. Roads had to be cleared by manual labour and sorties on to the moor to rescue buried sheep were frequent. The Flemings and their neighbours wisely made a habit of laying in extra stores to see them through the winter.

Darvel being four miles away, the farming families of the moor depended upon themselves for a change of company. Many a week, their only contact with Darvel civilization was when the postman called with letters and the daily paper. The Flemings and the Loudons of Overmoor were good neighbours and good friends. The link was strengthened even more by the marriage of Hugh, the master of Lochfield, to Kate Loudon. Not solely for the benefit of the children, the Loudons and the Flemings held parties alternately in each other's homes. Often, the visitors stayed the night.

Hallowe'en was particularly popular with the Fleming and Loudon families. There was no greater fun for children and adults than making toffee and dooking for apples in the smoky light of turnip lanterns or, as they were called locally, bouets.

The building which was Loudounmoor School. It is now a private dwelling.

All through his life, Alexander Fleming affirmed that the best of his education was obtained at Loudounmoor, the wee school which had been built in the early 1880s to serve the local farming families. Under the gentle care of teachers like Martha Aird, Elizabeth Tarbet and Elizabeth Haddow, the Fleming and Loudon children and their neighbours learned the Three Rs with a thoroughness which, as Alec readily admitted, allowed them to launch out confidently upon an academic career.

Discipline was a yoke which rested lightly upon the children of Loudounmoor School. When the weather was fine, classes were more often than not held in the open-air. Inspectors from Ayr ventured rarely on to the moor and, when they did, there was always plenty of time for the children to get back into the classroom before the 'foreigners,' as they were called, appeared.

Loudounmoor and its delightfully-human teachers were so beloved of Alec and Robert that, when the school came to the end of its 'glorious' days as a teaching establishment, they shared the cost of its purchase and turned it into a holiday home. One of the changes they made was to replace a fireplace with one built of stones which they gathered from the Glen Water.

The fireplace in Loudounmoor built with stones gathered by Sir Alexander and brother Robert from Glen Water.

Alec and Robert proceeded from Loudounmoor to Darvel School. It was here that Alec sustained a broken nose after colliding head-on with a classmate. Since he didn't suffer much, it wasn't thought necessary to set the break, and

Alec lived the rest of his life with the flat nose of a boxer.

Alec's stay at Darvel School was short, as was his subsequent stay at Kilmarnock Academy. From all accounts, he was well above average in his classwork without ever establishing himself at the top. His innate brilliance was still to develop fully.

The need to travel to Darvel and Kilmarnock developed in Alex a degree of physical endurance which few, if any, of his contemporaries could ever match. To attend Darvel School meant a round trip of eight miles a day on foot. Winter's severity often prevented him from making the trip, and, on these occasions, Robert and he would stay overnight with an old lady, Grace Morton, in Priestland. The brothers learned in later life that Grace was their mother's aunt and that she had also been born on Bransfield Farm.

In the years when Alec was growing from childhood into boyhood, 1881 - 1894, the town still depended on gas and oil for lighting. Probably the first time electricity was used was when Hood and Morton installed their own generators. That would be about 1893. "Magic," was how Robert described his feelings when Alec and he were allowed to switch the lights on and off.

Cottage craftsmen in those latter years of last century were finding securer employment in the new lace factories which were being built.

Public transport at that time meant the horse brake which plied from Darvel to connect with the railway at Newmilns; extension of the railway to Darvel being in the course of construction.

Though a natural environment forced the Flemings and other moorland families to live in isolation, they were not unknown in the Darvel community. Many of their contemporaries, indeed, were familiar to them by repute, if not in person.

Alexander (Big San) Morton, who introduced the power loom into the Valley, was well known to Mrs Fleming.

There was crotchety, but lovable old Angus McPherson of Gateside Farm, "Kennie Donal," the cadger or travelling grocer, the teachers at Loudounmoor, Uncle John at Ploughland, the Loudons of Overmoor.

There were so many Mortons that personal tags were needed to differentiate between them. There was Big San, his brother Wee Rab, his cousin, Hastings San, and Guy Morton, son of Wee Rab and founder of BMK, the world-famous carpet firm.

Nicol Jamieson, the butcher, had a business acquaintanceship with the Flemings. Then there was Dr Service, and Peter Craig and Peter Gorrie, both headmasters of Darvel School, Jean Fleming, or "Auntie Jean," unfailing and ungrudging dispenser of jeelie pieces to countless weans, and Cutty Smith, a local footballer who joined Glasgow Rangers and brought fame to Darvel by playing for Scotland.

This was the town of Darvel, then, which was "Big City" to the community at Lochfield. The Flemings were to remember it with growing affection in exile. Kinship between man and his birth-land was symbolically sealed when Alec returned as Sir Alexander in 1946 to have the Freedom of the Burgh conferred upon him.

Tom had already been some time in London, struggling to establish himself in general medical practice, when John joined him. Alec was hardly fourteen years old, Robert only twelve, when they, too, arrived and joined their brothers.

With Tom providing accommodation – usually this was in the house where he practised – the Lochfield colonists footslogged their way round London, mapping out their new urban territory as instinctively as animals of the field do and possibly for the same reason, security of mind and tenure.

Having dug themselves in, John, Alec and Robert looked around for work. John and Robert found places with an optical firm. Later, having made themselves proficient in optical engineering and manufacture, they set up together in business and were sucessful enough to establish a high reputation abroad as well as at home.

Alec by now was studying at the Polytechnic School in Regent Street, and it was here that the first evidence was seen of the brilliant career in store for him. In those days, Scottish elementary education was unquestionably the best that could be obtained in Britain. Based upon his age, Alec was placed well down the school when he started. His rise was rapid. Inside a week or two, he was moved up four classes and found himself the youngest pupil in the top class but one.

By the time Alec was sixteen, he had passed through the School with time to spare. He now had to look for work to assist in the upkeep of the household and this he found in a shipping office as a junior clerk. He had no great liking for his work but he carried out his duties to the best of his ability and consoled himself with the knowledge that he was gaining experience which might be useful later on.

During the time when the Fleming brothers were together in London, they were looked after successively by their sisters Mary and Gracie, another example of the responsibility unselfishly accepted by the Fleming women so that the men could follow their separate careers with undivided attention.

Tom's personal problems did not prevent him from keeping a senior and supervising eye on his younger brothers. In common with his mother, Tom realized that Alec possessed extraordinary talent and potential, and that clerical labour was no fulfilment for him nor ever could be. Mrs Fleming and Tom had ambitious plans for Alec: all that was needed was an opportunity to put them into practice.

Alec was twenty when Uncle John died and left him a handsome legacy of £250. Here was the opportunity Tom had been waiting for. The bequest coupled with an improvement in his own practice encouraged him to suggest to Alec that he use the money to set himself off on a medical career. The suggestion met with ready acceptance. Thus it was that Alec began the career which was to rank his name with such medical giants as Pasteur and Ehrlich and to bring him honour and adulation throughout the world.

How to get started in medicine was now the problem. Possessing none of the qualifications needed for entry upon a course at university or medical school, Fleming decided to start with medical school and work his way up to university standard. The pent-up talent inside Fleming was about to gush.

A short private course of instruction was all that Fleming needed to take first place in the examination of the Senior College of Preceptors. That was in July 1901. Suitably qualified now for entry to Medical School, Fleming sized up the twelve London teaching hospitals. Which was it to be? It is one of the countless myths which grew up around Fleming and encouraged him in late life to keep a special file for them, that his choice of St Mary's Hospital was dictated by the frivolous fact that he had once played water polo against a hospital team. As a private in the London Scottish Regiment, he had certainly taken to the water against St Mary's but his reason for entering the hospital medical school was more likely one of convenience. St Mary's happened to be nearest to his place of residence when he passed the qualifying examination.

The St Mary's which Fleming entered in October 1901 was a gloomy enough place but teaching was of a very high standard. His capacity for work and his almost complete freedom from fatigue, qualities bred into him at Lochfield, allowed him to follow a distinguished, prize-winning career at St Mary's and, at the same time, pass the matriculation examination for London University. Once again, Fleming took first place as he was to do in every other examination he was to sit. An acute awareness of what was going on around him, a natural inclination to listen and observe rather than indulge in self-projection, developed in him the ability not only to learn from his teachers but to note their preferences in subject matter and so be able, with a high rate of success, to guess the line their examinations would take. This, plus a faultless memory, an ability to ignore all but the essential features of lectures and handout information, saved Fleming valuable time all his life and gave him a high absorption rate in the assimilation of knowledge.

In 1906, he joined the team of St Mary's Inoculation Department under the celebrated bacteriologist, Almroth Wright. The course his life was to take had finally been set. Fleming took the Conjoint Qualification of London University in 1906 and the University's degree of MB BS in 1908. A year later, he passed the final examination of the Royal College of Surgeons and took the degree of FRCS. By now, he was looking to medical research as his supreme fulfilment.

The union of the separate, distinctive and sometimes conflicting geniuses of Wright and Fleming established the pattern which was to dominate therapeutic medicine in Britain, and to influence it in many other countries, for close on fifty years.

How these two great men, so different from each other in so many respects but sharing a passionate faith in medicine and themselves, met is a story which is very much in character with Fleming's theory that the course of his life was dictated by fate. It happened this way ....

Dr John Freeman had become obsessed with the idea of restoring some of its past glory to the ailing St Mary's Rifle Club. Looking around for recruits, he was referred to Alec Fleming who, as a result of enlistment in the London-Scottish on the outbreak of the Boer War, had attained a high degree of proficiency as a marksman. Freeman was warned of a strong possibility that Fleming might have to leave St Mary's to further his career.

At that time, Fleming was still showing an interest in surgery, but had little hope of immediate appointment to the surgical unit because others on the lookout for vacancies had longer service than he had. Freeman, therefore, had good reason to think that Fleming would leave St Mary's and that his prowess with a rifle would be denied the Rifle Club.

Freeman's approach to Fleming was received non-commitally, not an unhopeful sign in itself, since it allowed him to press his suggestion that Fleming should join Wright's Inoculation Department.

Sir Almroth Wright.

The desperate state of St Mary's Rifle Club was now reported to the 'Chief' with all the advocacy Freeman could muster. Fleming was a very good shot, he said – and a very good scientist. Why not give him a job in the Department?

In no way fooled by Freeman, rather amused by his duplicity, Wright allowed himself to be persuaded. Fleming was saved for St Mary's Rifle Club and so for its Inoculation Department.

Born in 1861 of an Irish father and a Swedish mother, Wright was a brilliant bacteriologist. Physically, he was a man of generous bulk, deliberate in movement, but sharp as a razor intellectually. His hands were big in keeping with his bulk but so sensitive as to allow him to use the most delicate laboratory equipment. Opinionative and provocative, Wright sparkled as a leader both in the laboratory and in the teatime exchange of views which he had daily with his staff in a box room, euphemistically dubbed 'the library.' In debate and conversation, he was positive and witty, well-rounded in expression, able to quote the classics from memory whenever he needed to ram home a point of argument.

His assistants held him in a kind of reverential awe. Never would he deny anyone the right to free research, even though he disagreed with the findings, but, at the same time, never did he shy clear of hard criticism if he thought an assistant had merited it. He was a mass of complexities and contradictions, scientist and poet, angel and devil. Almroth Wright was an amalgam of everything that Man ever was, a mixture of all things that have an opposite, but forgivably possessed of infinitely more virtue than imperfection.

Wright was thirty years old in 1891 when he was appointed Chief Pathologist in the Army School of Medicine at Netley Hospital. By now, medical science had established bacteria as a prime source of infection in humans. Bacteriological research laboratories were searching for Ehrlich's 'magic bullets,' the chemicals which, they were convinced, would destroy invading bacteria without harming the cells of the body. Ehrlich and other research bacteriologists like Wright believed that the 'magic bullets,' once found, would home in upon the target bacteria.

At Netley, Wright devoted much of his time to searching for a means of immunising against typhoid, a disease which was common in the Army and very much more so in time of war. Observing that blood after inoculation killed up to fifty times more bacteria than before and that it remained active for many months, Wright urged the War Office in 1898 to have every soldier vaccinated before going overseas.

The War Office did not reject Wright's advice out of hand but their decree that only soldiers who volunteered could be inoculated so offended Wright that he resigned his Netley post.

The medical assistants who came to serve in St Mary's Inoculation Department after Wright's appointment in 1902 were all men of superlative quality. Wright had already established a high reputation for himself in bacteriology, hence the unconcealed anxiety of students, in spite of his forbidding manner, to serve under him. Wright's first team included Bernard Spilsbury who, as Home Office Pathologist was later to become famous as a key crown witness in many notorious murder trials. John Freeman, another member of that first team, made an excellent reputation for himself as a writer on scientific subjects.

This was the quality of the men who were to be Fleming's laboratory companions when he joined the team in 1906. Shy, reserved, given to keeping to himself and getting on with his work, Fleming might have been excused for turning tail and running away. Nothing of the kind happened. The Wright regimentation attracted, rather than frightened him, a fact which is perhaps not difficult to understand when it is remembered that he came from a Scottish society which taught obedience to the father as a right not to be doubted or questioned.

Fleming found his companions stimulating, and, though he had expressed reservations in his earlier student days about Wright's teaching, he developed a solid and profound respect for the man. Wright's immensity, his 'larger than lifeness,' must have seemed grotesque to Fleming, but he had the ideal armoury for protection – full control of his emotions and the ability to withdraw into his own inviolable world of the mind.

The future was to produce occasions when Fleming would find himself disagreeing with Wright's views and theories and would openly say so. Fleming's highly-developed sense of loyalty always ensured that any differences he had with Wright were expressed solely within the team, never in the world outside.

Wright attracted men of high calibre. Women were anathema to him, though one suspects that there was more mischief than malice in his misogyny for, from all accounts, he lacked none of the qualities of a good husband.

St Mary's under the influence of Wright was becoming well known for its work on vaccine therapy by the time Fleming arrived. The famous tea-parties in St Mary's 'library' were graced by many famous men – statesmen like Arthur Balfour and John Burns, biologists like Ehrlich and Metchnikoff, and dramatists like George Bernard Shaw and Granville Barker. Wright was the attraction for the famous, and they all warmed themselves deliciously in the glory reflected from one to the other. Fleming sat silent – listening and absorbing.

One day when Shaw was visiting, there was some talk about what would happen if more patients came to Wright's clinic than his staff could cope with. Pressed by Shaw to give answer, Wright said it would have to be decided whom it was best to save. The drama was not lost upon Shaw, for he went off and wrote his famous play, "The Doctor's Dilemma," and put Almroth Wright into the skin of the leading character, Sir Colenso Ridgeon.

Wright's knighthood was the result of both personal merit and influential acquaintance. Lord Haldane, Secretary of State for War, wrote to Wright, saying that his Typhoid Prophylactic was needed for the Army but that the Army medical chief did not agree. Wright had to have his public image built up if the Prophylactic was to be accepted. As a first step Wright had to be knighted, said Haldane.

Fleming came to St Mary's clothed in medical honours, and, in time he was to make a massive contribution to the work of the Inoculation Department. His habit of silence was misleading, and Wright had early knowledge of this. Fleming proved to be as expressive and as clear in exposition as he was in devizing and constructing laboratory apparatus. This love of listening could not suddenly give way to loquaciousness, but, when Fleming was silent in company, that always meant he was learning and he showed his learning on paper. In his hands, too, primitive pieces of equipment could be made to meet the requirements of the most complicated and delicate experiments. There was engineering skill in his laboratory work, showing an artistry which had first revealed itself in the fashioning of clay.

Fleming's laboratory at St Mary's.

Fleming, 'little Flem,' as he was often affectionately called, established himself at St Mary's both as a scientist and as a person. Ever ready to listen, he was well equipped to help out with someone else's problems. In his student days and in his teaching days, his door was always open to anyone who called. Official appointments were seldom needed to gain access to Fleming. There was a presence about him which put callers at their ease and made them feel they were honouring him by seeking his company and advice.

Robert Fleming recalls that Alec sometimes committed things to memory with the aid of mnemonics. A favourite with Alec went like this:

> "If you want the bowels to go,
> Try rhubarb, ginger, MgO:
> But, if you want a regular starter,
> Try jalop, ginger and cream of tartar."

As so many great men do, Fleming felt the need of a little nonsense now and again.

Wright was paymaster as well as principal in St Mary's Inoculation Department. Money for research was hard to come by, but the shortage was offset in various ways and, in the end, was more of an inspiration to the team than a hardship.

It was insisted by Wright that his assistants should engage in private practice. There were various good reasons for this. Much of the money which kept the Department running came out of Wright's own pocket, part of the profit he made from a private practice which had attracted many wealthy and influential patients. Salaries for his assistants were fixed by him at £100, hardly big enough to allow them to survive without the proceeds of some other form of professional activity.

Wright's dictum was that the best research would be done by workers who did not expect to earn full subsistence from their labour – hence his requirement that assistants should follow him in private practice. He also contended, with some wisdom, that contact with the sick was a good thing for scientists who were looking for cures. All of Wright's assistants, including Fleming, accepted his nominal remuneration without complaint, and eked it out, never in any luxurious style, in the manner he had suggested. Not that Fleming or any of his colleagues required Wright or anyone else to teach them a moral code. All of them had come into research and had chosen to work under Wright for reasons which transcended cash remuneration.

Indeed in 1912, Fleming, according to his brother, Robert, took a consulting room in Devonshire Place. His reputation so firmly established him that, had he wanted to do so, he could have built up a very wealthy practice. Events relieved him of the need to make up his mind whether or not to follow this path. The chances were that his continuing connection with St Mary's and his obsessive interest in research would have persuaded him to give up practice. Be that as it may, when war with Germany broke out in 1914, Fleming finished up at Devonshire Place and was never seen again in the role of G.P.

Much of the work at St Mary's was routine — daily rounds of the wards, analysis of samples taken from patients, both those who were resident in hospital and those who attended Wright's clinic. Ardent disciples of the gospel of therapeutic vaccination, the team turned no one away and they gave a particular welcome to those suffering from conditions regarded by other medical people as hopeless. The doctors often used their own blood as the control when analysing samples taken from patients.

Not surprisingly, the extraordinary growth of public interest which was now being shown in Wright's Inoculation Department had put an unbearable strain upon accommodation from the Hospital Authority — two small, overcrowded rooms. Accepting an offer of more accommodation from the Hospital Authority, Wright raised the money needed to develop it for his needs and make his Department more or less independent. This was about 1909. The year before, Fleming had added to his considerable list of academic honours by passing his final medical examinations and winning the Gold Medal of the University of London.

Fleming's progress continued to gather momentum. By now, Wright had come to regard him with the kind of respect he habitually reserved for those of similar calibre to himself. He had a profound respect for Fleming's acute powers of observation and the clinical thoroughness he showed in interpretation.

Very sure of himself now, very sure of his methods of research, his deductions, and his conclusions, Fleming was beginning to make himself widely known. As a contributor to medical journals, he displayed clarity and expressive force which proved that his reticence was certainly not the result of a deficiency in articulation.

The appearance of Salvarsan in 1910 was important beyond measure to Fleming. First of the 'magic bullets,' Salvarsan had been successfully used by its discoverer, Ehrlich, to cure syphilitic lesions. Because of his association with the staff of St Mary's, the Hospital was one of the few hospitals outside Germany to be given a sample of Salvarsan for test. Fleming was chosen along with Dr Colebrook to carry out this work.

Salvarsan in the hands of Fleming and Colebrook did all that Ehrlich claimed for it. There was a miraculous efficiency about the way it cleared up syphilis. Together, the two St Mary's doctors affirmed their faith in Salvarsan in an article in Lancet. Fleming was more convinced than ever that substances existed which would destroy pathogenic bacteria in the human body without destroying its natural protectors, the phagocytes.

Outbreak of the 1914-18 war with Germany saw Fleming in the role of officer in the Royal Army Medical Corps. Immediately the shooting had begun, the War Office sent Wright to Boulogne charged with establishing a laboratory for research into wound infections. The unit was eventually set up in the local Casino: with natural military efficiency, Wright 'mobilized' Douglas, Morgan, Fleming, Colebrook and Freeman from St Mary's. Fleming, whose rank had been no higher than private in his London-Scottish days, found himself raised to the rank of Lieutenant and then to Captain in the Royal Army Medical Corps.

Fleming, then a captain in the Royal Army Medical Corps, is seen in his laboratory in Boulogne Casino.

Man's ingenuity as a creator of weapons which destroy him in greater quantity, greater pain and greater disfiguration filled hospitals and clearing-stations with butchered, suppurating and necrotic flesh in mass. This shambles was to be place of work and home for the St Mary's medical team.

Lister had shown the value of antiseptics in hospital operating theatres, how they could sterilize instruments, walls, and floors, and keep the surgeon's hands clean. How to control and get rid of wound infection, however, was still not known and it was still a common belief that antiseptics could accomplish the task.

This was the latest medical thinking on antiseptics when the Boulogne Unit was set up. Fleming hardly needed his great powers of observation to see that antiseptics were having no beneficial effect on infected wounds and that some were actually making the infection worse, more readily killing the human leucocytes than the microbial cells, and adding to the victim's pain. Antiseptics, neither in quantity nor variety, made any difference to the death-rate from war wounds.

Fleming was justifiably proud of his work on antiseptics. Using various antiseptics against various infections, he showed that the antiseptics were not just ineffective but could actually increase infection.

When the war ended in November 1918, there was still no adequate remedy against wound infection. Ehrlich's 'magic bullet' was still the only one – and this was effective against only one disease.

The genius of Alexander Fleming which had been manifesting itself sporadically since he joined St Mary's in 1902 came into full flower between 1918 and 1928. In these ten years, he was to discover lysozyme, a natural anti-biotic found in human tissue and secretions, and widely dispersed throughout the natural, living world, and finally, in triumphant justification of his own long-held, passionate beliefs, he was to uncover penicillin and release its countless, curative properties to Mankind.

Fleming, as has been said, did not start up again in private practice after the war ended. His calling was to research and so he returned to St Mary's, to his laboratory, and to Wright.

His Lochfield experience continued to uphold him. He required little sleep, never seemed to get tired, and, no matter how late he had worked the night before, he was usually first to start work in the morning. St Mary's and his laboratory were another home to him. He owed much to the influence of his mother that he had been enabled to take up a profession which was intellectually exciting and satisfying. He was very much the inspired son of an inspiring mother. Now, as he crossed the threshold into what was to be the place of supreme fulfilment for him, he was to lean heavily upon a second remarkable woman for the support he needed to pursue his ambition.

Fleming was in his 35th year when he married Sarah McElroy, daughter of a farmer in County Mayo, on 23 December, 1915. One of four sisters, all of whom were nurses, Sarah (or Sareen as she later asked to be called) was running a private nursing home in York Place when Fleming and she became acquainted.

Like her husband, Sareen was devoted to her profession. Yet, realizing that his work was more important in direction and promise than hers, she subordinated herself willingly and entirely.

Convinced that Fleming had greatness in store for him, Sareen set herself the duty of complementing his life with her own. They were very different from each other in many respects but, far from weakening their alliance, it tended to add strength to it. Sareen's exuberance and vivaciousness counter-acted her husband's silence and aloofness: both understood and respected each other and, as a couple, they were never without friends.

Surrounded by friends at London-Ayrshire Society Functions.

With characteristic unselfishness, Sareen sold her nursing home to ease the financial strain which her husband was feeling and thus allow him to give undivided attention to his work. Using the money she obtained from the sale, Sareen purchased a charming country cottage called, The Dhoon, at Barton Mills in Suffolk. Together, they spent many happy years shaping the garden ground to their own taste, and setting it with an abundance of fruit, flower and vegetable. Fleming enjoyed the added pleasure of fishing on a private stretch of river which flowed through the grounds of The Dhoon.

Sareen made up for the want of servants by matching her husband's industry in the laboratory with similar industry in and around the home. She did all the household chores and, at the same time, kept the garden tidy and productive.

The Dhoon was holiday home to the Flemings for the rest of their lives together. When their son, Robert, was born in December 1924, Sareen started the habit of repairing with him and some nephews to The Dhoon for the summer months. In London, the Flemings lived in an equally-attractive house which Fleming had leased in Danvers Street, Chelsea, and which became a popular howf or ca' hoose with local artists whose company Fleming liked to cultivate.

The Dhoon.

Sir Alexander, brother Robert and sister-in-law Ida relax in the garden at The Dhoon.

Secure in his private life, freed by the resourcefulness and devotion of his wife, Fleming quickly settled again into his familiar routine at St Mary's once the war had ended.

Thanks to generous gifts from Lord Revelstoke and Lord Beaverbrook, the Medical School was completely modernized with great benefit to staff, patients and student doctors. Fleming was given his own laboratory overlooking Praed Street. In 1921, Wright appointed him assistant Director of the Department of Pathology and Research (the new name for the Inoculation Department). St Mary's and he were now prepared for the great events which were looming not so far ahead.

An attack of the common cold in 1921 led Fleming to discovery of a substance which, he was later to prove, exists in living matter to protect it against contamination. It is an ill wind, indeed, that blaws naebody guid.'

Hunched over an agar plate on which colonies of a contaminant had grown, Fleming was astounded to see them disappear when a drip from his nose landed in their midst. The phenomenon was immediately and correctly interpreted by him as proof that nasal mucus contained a substance which could destroy microbial organisms, a substance which, in medical terms, could effect lysis.

With natural tenacity, Fleming followed up his discovery and established that lysozyme, the Greek name he gave to the new substance, existed in tears and saliva, in phagocytes, skin and fingernails, in human milk, in the lower animals and in plants.

In a published paper, Dr Amalia Coutsouri-Voureka, who was to be Fleming's second wife, draws attention to the delight which discovery of lysozyme gave to Fleming. "He had two great reasons to cherish lysozyme," she writes. "It was the first antiseptic he had studied during long years of hard work and search which fulfilled what he required of a bactericidal substance, namely, that it should be selectively more lethal to bacteria than to human cells. What was dearer to Fleming's heart — lysozyme was, as he proved, part of the human cells, of the whole body's natural resistance."

Dr Coutsouri-Voureka draws attention to the relationship

between lysozyme and penicillin. "It would be right to say that lysozyme made the discovery of penicillin easier," she writes. "Both substances have very much in common. They were discovered in almost an identical way. To study penicillin, Fleming used the methods he had devized to study lysozyme."

Significant though Fleming's discovery was, lysozyme was greeted with cold indifference when he came to read papers on it before the Medical Research Club and the Royal Society. The response left a mark on his sensitivity, but he tholed the pain and stepped up the work he was putting out on lysozyme. "We shall hear more about it," he would say again and again.

In collaboration with Dr Allison, Fleming established that, while lysozyme was able to kill some bacteria without harming leucocytes, its action on bacteria producing morbid or diseased conditions was very weak.

"This was natural," writes Dr Coutsouri-Voureka. "Otherwise, the bacteria would not have been able to establish themselves in the body and be pathogenic. They would have been killed by lysozyme. Fleming thought that the definition of a pathogenic germ was that it was resistant to lysozyme."

Already aware of the bactericidal qualities of egg-white, Fleming established by experiment that its concentration of lytic elements was 100 times higher than in tears. Tests for toxicity on leucocytes and bacteria in this higher egg-white concentration showed that lysozyme was still harmless to leucocytes but that it now had a marked effect on pathogenic bacteria. Intravenous injections of egg-white solution into rabbits did not upset them but enhanced the bactericidal power of their blood.

Fleming and Allison laboured to produce lysozyme in pure form so that it could be administered to human beings, but, as Fleming was to find with penicillin, a lack of adequate knowledge of chemistry prevented them from succeeding.

"Fleming had struggled in the First World War to find an antiseptic which would help prevent and cure the infection of wounds," Dr Coutsouri-Voureka goes on. "He had dreamt that Nature, this Nature he believed so much in, must have provided every living thing with an effective defence mechanism which would protect it in all its parts. With his discovery of lysozyme, Fleming believed he had found this primeval natural defence mechanism. He had also found something much greater: he had found hope."

Fleming published six papers on lysozyme, five of them in collaboration with Allison. Between the year of its discovery, 1921, and its extraction in pure form by Dr Roberts of Oxford in 1937, lysozyme became a more and more familiar subject of published comment in the medical world.

"We will hear more of lysozyme," Fleming had prophesied. Today, lysozyme is used in the protection of foods and for the treatment of internal and eye infections. When added to cow's milk, it reproduces the component structure of human milk. By dissolving the mucins which cover microbes, lysozyme makes the work of the bacteriologist easier.

Fleming's prophecy for lysozyme is coming true.

Dr Coutsouri-Voureka was absolutely right when she wrote that Fleming's discovery of lysozyme made his later discovery of penicillin easier. Having seen his nose-drip dissolve contaminants on an agar plate, Fleming was unlikely to ignore another phenomenon which occurred in his Praed-Street laboratory in 1928.

Fleming had a habit of holding on to cultures until he was satisfied he had nothing more to learn from them. Possibly with a mind to tidying up at last, he was examining some cultures when he noticed that, while moulds covered them all, one of the cultures was different. Whereas all the other moulds existed tolerantly with colonies of staphylococci, the one which had attracted Fleming's attention had dissolved the staphylococci immediately surrounding it and the process was advancing steadily into the remaining colonies.

Fleming's own account of that historic moment of discovery, as given by him in an address to the Ayrshire Division of the British Medical Association, can be appropiately interpolated at this stage. The account appears in the Kilmarnock Standard of 29 July 1944.

"You all know that penicillin is a substance made by a mould," he said. "There are thousands of moulds, and there is one class of them called Penicillium. It was my good fortune once that one particular Penicillium blew on to a culture-plate I was playing with — the beginning, I suppose, of penicillin.

"There were lots of microbes on this plate. It had been lying about on the bench of my laboratory for a week or two, and I had forgotton about it. The mould had got on to it, and I found that a lot of microbes had disappeared — a funny sort of thing."

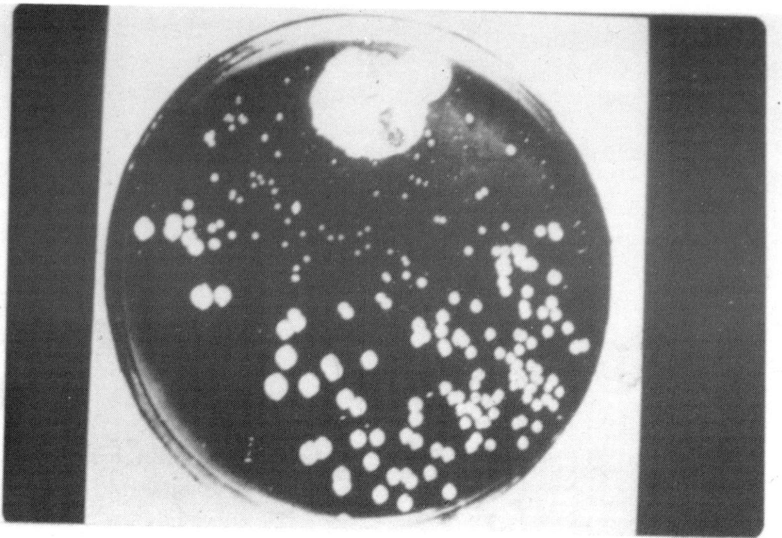

The famous Fleming photograph showing the action of the mould PENICILLIUM NOTATUM on colonies of staphylococci.

Removing a section of the strange mould, Fleming set it in a dish of agar and grew a second colony. Excited about the bactericidal potential of the mould, he cultivated it next in a broth and obtained a yellow liquid from the process. Tests showed that the liquid was as active as the mould in attacking bacteria. Even diluted to 1/500th of its original strength, the liquid was capable of inhibiting development in staphylococci. Fleming suspected by now that he was in contact with a substance which had remarkable bactericidal and bacteriostatic powers.

What was the identity of the substance? What, first of all, was the identity of the mould? PENICILLIUM RUBRUM was the first guess, PENICILLIUM CHRYSOGENUM the next. Neither was right. Correct identification – PENICILLIUM NOTATUM – was made by an American mycologist, Dr Thom. PENICILLIN was Fleming's choice of name for the antibiotic substance he so desperately wanted to track down and harness.

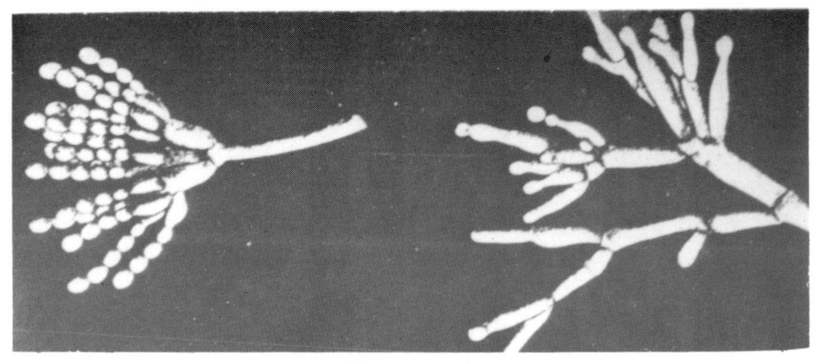

Spore of Penicillium Notatum.

As had happened after his discovery of lysozyme, Fleming found himself severely restricted in his work on penicillin by his relatively poor knowledge of chemistry. Wright had little respect for chemists and opposed their recruitment to his staff. In those circumstances, Fleming had either to pursue his work on his own, or with assistants who were often no more skilled in chemistry than he was, or rely upon help from outside sources.

Fleming at work in St Mary's laboratory.

The instability which was immediately evident in penicillin added to the difficulty of isolating it in pure form. Failure attended attempts by Fleming and an assistant, Dr Stuart Craddock, to produce penicillin first of all from a culture of the mould in broth and then from a culture of the mould in milk. Nevertheless, Fleming was able to show not only that the mould juice was a powerful antibiotic but that it was also non-toxic to animals.

Dr Ridley, who had worked on lysozyme, joined Fleming and Craddock, but the trio were no more successful. Penicillin's instability continued to thwart all attempts to isolate it.

Still unperturbed, convinced, as always, that all experience, even defeat and disappointment, can be constructive, Fleming published an up-to-date report on penicillin in the British Journal of Experimental Pathology. The report is important for, in it, he records that a certain type of penicillin produces in culture a powerful anti-bacterial substance and that penicillin, even in massive doses, is non-toxic to animals. It was the first detailed, scientific report on an antibiotic.

Response to Fleming's published report was hardly enthusiastic. Nor was the response he received to a paper which he delivered at the Medical Research Club. On this latter occasion, Fleming was sensitively reminded of the Club's cold reception of his address on lysozyme.

At this stage, several other attempts were made to solve the problem of instability. A team led by Harold Raistrick, a prominent English biochemist, carried the fight a stage further by cultivating the mould in a synthetic medium. Though the anti bacterial substance showed up in ether, it disappeared whenever attempts were made to harvest it by evaporating the liquid. The same result was obtained by Dr Holt, a biochemist, after he had managed to expose penicillin in an acetate solution.

The Holt attempt on penicillin was made in 1934 and was to be the last before the fugitive was finally caught and controlled in 1940. Fleming concealed his disappointment over the failures by constantly reaffirming his faith in penicillin as an antibiotic and his belief that it would eventually be harnessed. Attempts by Fleming to test the curative properties of penicillin juice in hospital were defeated by the now-familiar instability which took over before the substance could do effective work.

Appearance of the sulphonamides in the 1930s supported the theory that there were substances which were selectively more lethal to bacterial cells than to human ones, as penicillin had already proved to be. Addressing the Royal Society of Medicine, Fleming showed that the sulphonamides, while effective against some bacteria, had no effect on others, that they had little or no antibacterial power when faced with large numbers of microbes, that they were bacteriostatic, not bactericidal, and required, therefore, the help of the body's natural defences to finish off the bacteria.

Fleming followed up his public assessment of the sulphonamides by setting up a series of experiments designed to compare them with penicillin as bactericidal substances. Sulphonamides he found very effective against weak microbial dilutions but powerless to inhibit non-diluted cultures. Penicillin, on the other hand, was effective in every case, but, because it was still unstable, it would have to give best to the sulphonamides which were both stable and pure.

Just as the First World War had stimulated the study of antiseptics, so the war of 1939-45 provided the drive which was to lead to the production of pure penicillin.

It is more than possible that Fleming was unaware of the work which began at Oxford University just before the 1939-45 war broke out and ended triumphantly with the production of pure penicillin. Failure of Dr Holt's attempt in 1934 persuaded Fleming to devote more time to other research, at the same time, of course, maintaining his faith in penicillin and the conviction that it would eventually be produced in pure form.

Three years later, in 1937, Dr Ernst Chain, a German biochemist, who had come to England when Hitler came to power, accepted an invitation to work in the Biochemical Department at Oxford under Dr Howard Florey, an Australian pathologist

With Florey's approval, Chain began a study of Fleming's 1929 paper on penicillin. Attracted by Fleming's conclusions, the two Oxford men decided to make another attempt to obtain pure penicillin. The Rockefeller Foundation weighed in with a contribution of 5000 dollars towards the work.

The war had just begun when Chain, with the help of Dr Heatley, finally made the breakthrough which had been denied Fleming, Ridley, Craddock, Raistrick and others. Using the newly-discovered method of lyophilisation, Chain obtained enough pure penicillin to allow biological tests to be carried out by Florey. Results were spectacular and decisive. Fifty mice were infected by streptococci and half were given regular injections of penicillin. At the end of 16 hours, 24 of the injected mice were still alive. All the others had died. Pure penicillin had at last been produced and tested successfully on animals. Later tests confirmed Fleming's findings that penicillin was a powerful antibiotic and non-toxic to human beings.

Fleming became aware of the work of Florey, Chain and Heatley when they published their findings in the Lancet in August 1940. A visit to Oxford established their first contact. It was to be renewed dramatically two years later.

The amazing curative properties of penicillin were generally and immediately recognized, and interest was heightened by the fact that war casualties were growing in number. But, for various reasons, not least being the fact that Britain, on her own now that France had capitulated to Germany, had more than enough to do surviving without taking up the production of penicillin. On top of that, the process which had been perfected at Oxford was not suited to production of the large quantities needed for treatment of war casualties.

The United States of America was an obvious choice for mass-production of penicillin; and so, off on a sales tour of the US went Florey and Heatley in June 1941. With them, they took some penicillin. Reaction initially was slow, but interest built up steadily, first of all in the American pharmaceutical industry and then within the Government.

The visit to the United States gave the production of penicillin the impetus that was needed. Florey and Heatley called at the Northern Regional Research Laboratory in Peoria, Illinois, and surprised the Americans by handing over to them the results of their work on penicillin. Leaving Heatley at Peoria, Florey went off on a solitary pilgrimage through US and Canada. The journey proved worthwhile, bringing him promises from two pharmaceutical firms to send his Oxford team enough penicillin for their work. More important, Florey had managed to arouse the interest of the US Government in production. Back in Peoria, Heatley saw the laboratory boost penicillin production 20-fold by using corn steep liquor and boost it still further by substituting lactose for glucose.

Mass-production was beginning, too, in Britain. Chain had continued his work on penicillin while Florey and Heatley were abroad. The first factory for the manufacture of penicillin had already been set up in Oxford.

Penicillin was tried successfully on war wounds and, in August, 1942, it had its most spectacular success. Fleming who was treating a director in his brothers' optical firm diagnosed the symptoms of meningitis. At his request, Florey supplied enough penicillin for full treatment. By the end of August, all signs of meningitis had left the patient and he was released from hospital a few days later.

PENICILLIN

TO THE EDITOR OF THE TIMES

Sir,—In the leading article on penicillin in your issue yesterday you refrained from putting the laurel wreath for this discovery round anybody's brow. I would, with your permission, supplement your article by pointing out that, on the principle *palmam qui meruit ferat*, it should be decreed to Professor Alexander Fleming of this research laboratory. For he is the discoverer of penicillin and was the author also of the original suggestion that this substance might prove to have important applications in medicine.

I am, Sir, yours faithfully,

ALMROTH E. WRIGHT.

Inoculation Department, St. Mary's Hospital, Paddington, W.2, Aug. 28. 1942

The cure was greeted by Lancet with a call to the British Government to start mass-production of penicillin at once. The Times wrote an enthusiastic leader without mentioning, Fleming, Florey, Chain or Heatley. Unselfishly, Wright composed a letter to the editor, crediting Fleming with the discovery of penicillin.

STREPTOCOCCAL MENINGITIS TREATED WITH PENICILLIN

MEASUREMENT OF BACTERIOSTATIC POWER OF BLOOD AND CEREBROSPINAL FLUID

ALEXANDER FLEMING, F R C S, F R S

PROFESSOR OF BACTERIOLOGY IN THE UNIVERSITY OF LONDON

(Inoculation Department, St. Mary's Hospital, Paddington)

THIS case was one of those recently reported by Florey and Florey.[1] It was then included (case 12) in a series with many others and therefore the notes had to be severely abridged. The case was the first in which intrathecal injection of penicillin was used, and the first in which the bacteriostatic power of the blood and spinal fluid was systematically titrated throughout the treatment, so that it seems worthy of a more complete record. More especially it seems important that the methods used for testing the bacteriostatic power of the blood and cerebrospinal fluid should be described, for there is as yet no chemical test for penicillin in blood as there is for the sulphonamides, and the only way of estimating the penicillin content of the blood is by bacteriostatic tests. More patients are now being treated with penicillin both here and in America, and it is very desirable that estimations of the bacteriostatic power of blood, &c. should be made so that the dosage of the drug can be scientifically controlled.

It may be that a favourable result in this case could have been obtained by intrathecal treatment only, but at that time penicillin had not been used in this manner, and there was no knowledge as to how it would be tolerated or for how long it would remain active in the spinal fluid. The observations made on this case have enabled other cases of meningitis to be treated successfully by local treatment with an enormous saving of penicillin—an important thing in these days of scarcity.

CLINICAL NOTES

Male, aged 52. Fever began June 18, 1942. No localising signs. Admitted to St. Mary's Hospital on July 7. Temp. 100·2° F. No satisfactory diagnosis could be made.

July 14. Developed signs indicating meningitis. Drowsy and wandering with slight neck-rigidity. Lumbar puncture

1. Florey, M. E. and Florey, H. W. *Lancet*, 1943, i, 387.

The Lancet report on the meningitis case.

Responding to an approach by Fleming, Sir Andrew Duncan, Minister of Supply, persuaded some British pharmaceutical companies to go ahead with mass-production. Penicillin was soon helping the Allies in North Africa and the Pacific. By 1943, enough penicillin was being produced to allow it to be used in the treatment of factory wounds.

Suddenly, Fleming, this shy, reticent, retiring little Scot, found himself a cynosure for the media. The secluded reservation which he had painstakingly built for himself was invaded by reporters, writers and commentators, all of them seeking to present the 'man of penicillin' in the role of some medical Saviour of the World.

Between 1945 and 1948, he was made a Freeman of Paddington where he worked, a Freeman of Chelsea where he lived, and a Freeman of Darvel where he was born.

Fleming often remarked that the most important of the three 'Freedom' ceremonies to him was the one at Darvel. The event which took place in the local Town Hall on Saturday, 26 October, 1946, was given 'splash' coverage in Kilmarnock Standard.

"Darvel honours scientist son," boomed the headline.

"Darvel had the air of being *en fete,*" said the Standard. "Most of the shops and factories, and many of the houses, were gay with flags and bunting. A vast crowd of people assembled in Hastings Square in front of the Town Hall prior to the hour fixed for the ceremony, and Darvel Burgh Band entertained them with lively music. When Sir Alexander and Lady Fleming and their son, Mr Robert Fleming (now Dr Fleming) arrived, they got a tumultuous welcome. Sir Alexander was obviously touched by the warmth of his reception."

The Standard notes that every seat in the Town Hall was occupied long before Sir Alexander and his entourage came in. Front rows were given over to the Senior Citizens of Darvel, and the balcony was occupied by guests who could not find a place on the platform.

"As famous as Lord Kelvin, Professor Curie and others who have made great improvements in medicine and surgery" – Provost David Paterson's tribute on behalf of Darvel people to their kinsman, Sir Alexander.

"From now on," said the Provost, "penicillin and Alexander Fleming will be synonymous terms. Wherever penicillin is spoken of, Fleming will be spoken of and Darvel will bask in reflected glory."

Provost Paterson recalled Sir Alexander's distinguished academic and professional career, and its culmination in "the phenomenal discovery of penicillin."

Dr Robert Hamilton, Kilmarnock, paid tribute to Sir Alexander on behalf of the doctors of Ayrshire. He had a timely warning, however, for those who, under the influence of press publicity, tended to regard penicillin as a panacea. "That is not the case," he said. "The choice of suitable subjects for administration of penicillin must be left to the physician or the surgeon."

Provost John Carnie of Kilmarnock hailed Sir Alexander as "great scientist, doctor, and public benefactor."

Presentation of Darvel's Burgess Ticket in a polished metal tube bearing the Burgh Coat of Arms was made to Sir Alexander by Provost Paterson. The Ticket records that "the Provost, Magistrates and Councillors of Darvel, receive and admit Sir Alexander Fleming to be a Burgess, with the whole liberties, privileges and immunities thereon belonging, in testimony of their high appreciation of the invaluable services rendered by him to Mankind by his scientific and medical researches culminating in the discovery of penicillin, and in appreciation of the ties of birthright existing between him and the Burgh of Darvel, and of the esteem and admiration which they hold for him personally."

Sir Alexander's local attachment came bubbling out of him as he acknowledged Darvel's tribute. Lochfield, Loudounmoor School., Darvel School – there was affection in his memories.

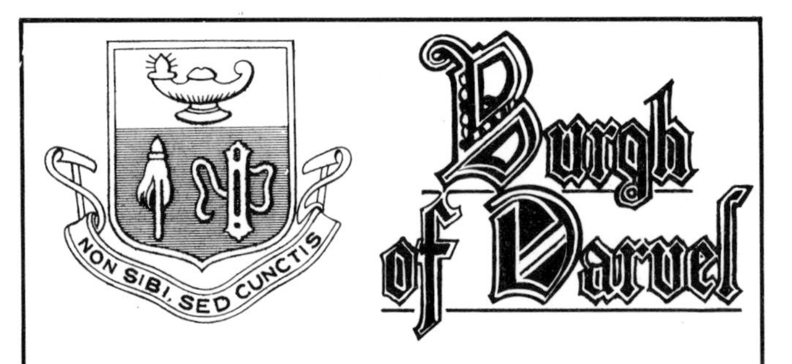

At Darvel the 26th day of October in the year one thousand nine hundred and forty-six, which day the Provost Magistrates & Councillors of the Burgh of Darvel being convened they receive and admit —

Sir Alexander Fleming, MB BS (London) FRCS FRCP FRS

to be a Burgess of the said Burgh with the whole liberties, privileges and immunites thereto belonging; in testimony of their high appreciation of the invaluable services rendered by him to mankind by his scientific and medical researches culminating in his discovery of penicillin; and in appreciation of the ties of birthright existing between him and the Burgh of Darvel; and of the esteem and admiration which they hold for him personally.

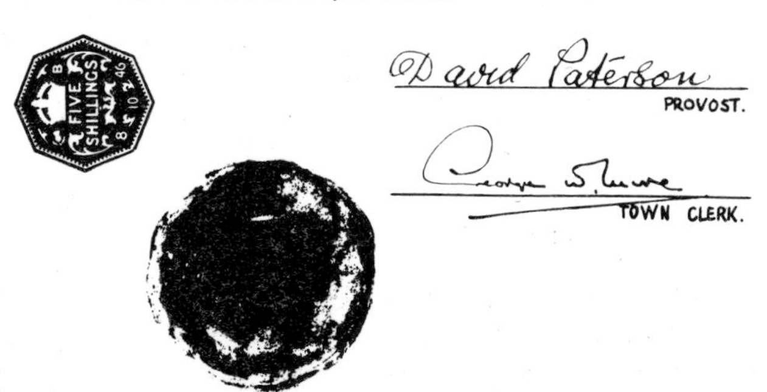

"I have not been in this countryside except for a few days now and then for many years," he said. "The people change, but the country is just the same. The same pools are in the burn, the same stones are there; and I have no doubt the decendants of the same trout we guddled as boys are under the same stones. It is all the same except for the human difference. It is a good country, and it was worth our forefathers fighting for. I am proud of it and I am glad you have received me back into the fold as a burgess of Darvel, the proudest title I could have. Darvel is my native town, and the Freedom of Darvel, therefore, has a very special significance for me."

The Standard ends on a grand note. "There was a great outburst of cheering as Sir Alexander sat down," said the report. "It swelled to a crescendo when Provost Paterson called for 'Three cheers for Darvel's youngest Burgess.' There was another roar of acclamation for Lady Fleming. The cheers were taken up by the great crowd which had stood in Hastings Square throughout the ceremony, listening to the speeches relayed by loud-speakers."

The Duke of Edinburgh hands over two silver soup tureens to Fleming to mark the 25th anniversary of the publication of the first Fleming paper on penicillin.

The freedom 'trilogy' introduced a decade in which honours were lavished upon Fleming. At St Mary's, his colleagues presented him with an 18th-Century silver salver. The Royal Society, which had shown no interest when he addressed them on lysozyme in 1922, made him a Fellow and so did the Royal College of Physicians.

Fleming, Chain and Florey at the presentation of the Nobel Prize for Medicine by the King of Sweden.

The year 1944 brought Fleming a Knighthood. In December 1945, he shared the Nobel Prize for Medicine with Florey and Chain, an honour which had much to do with his appointment as Principal of the Wright-Fleming Institute (this was the new name for the Inoculation Department) on the retiral of Wright in 1946. He was to serve as Principal for some nine years and, when it was time to lay aside the duty in 1955, the Society of Microbiology gave a dinner in his honour.

Edinburgh University elected him their Rector by an overwhelming majority in 1951. Among the many other home honours bestowed upon him were Fellowships from the Royal College of Physicians, London, the Royal College of Physicians, Edinburgh, and the Royal Society of Edinburgh. He was awarded the Gold Medal of the Royal College of Surgeons and the Addingham Medal.

The homage paid to Fleming at home was repeated on an even grander scale abroad. Academies, universities and institutes invited him on lecture tours and showered honours upon him. Governments decorated him with ribbon and medal. King and Queen, pontiff, president and prime minister granted him audience. Every journey for Fleming was a triumphal progress.

Sareen accompanied her husband on his travels until her health broke down in 1948. She was to live only a year longer. Fleming, who had been in the United States when war broke out in 1939, returned with Sareen in 1945 to be feted at New York's Waldorf by American penicillin manufacturers, and to receive an honorary medical degree from Harvard University. When he went back for the third time in 1949, it was to be made a member of the Kiowa tribe of Indians.

The Flemings visited France twice. In 1945, they were received by General de Gaulle as guests of the Government of France. Fleming was made a Member of L'Academie de Medicine. On his return to France three years later, he was made a Member of the Academie Septentrionale and sat for Baron who had been commissioned by the French Mint to design a medal celebrating the discovery of penicillin.

The year 1945 also took Fleming to Belgium to receive honorary degrees from the Universities of Brussels, Liege and Louvain, and to Stockholm to receive the Nobel Prize.

Sir Alexander and Lady Fleming in Belfast, 1944.

The gratitude of ordinary people went out to Fleming wherever he went, and he was emotionally affected by its warmth and sincerity.

Fleming's Spanish tour in 1948 brought him the close attention of the poorest people. More than most, perhaps, they knew the value of penicillin, and they made an emotional display of their gratitude to Fleming. To them, he was some kind of medical Messiah.

The Flemings had an audience with Queen Marie-Jose of Italy. University degrees, membership of various academies, and the Grand Cross of Alphonso the Wise were bestowed upon Fleming.

Sareen took ill in Madrid and, when Fleming resumed his travels, he was on his own for the first time. In 1949, Fleming travelled to Rome to be made a Member of the Pontifical Academy of Sciences and to meet the Pope.

Pope Pius XII receives Fleming in audience in The Vatican.

Later that same year, on 29 October, not long after Fleming returned from his third visit to the United States, Sareen died.

Sir Alexander and Lady Fleming in Madrid during their Spanish visit of 1948.

Sareen's death robbed Fleming of much of his natural vigour and vitality for some time. For 34 years, she had been by his side, willingly acting out the secondary but crucial roles of help-mate and advocate. In his desolation, he turned in upon himself, shutting off from the world of colleague and friend until he had adjusted to his new condition.

Invitations continued to pour in upon Fleming from abroad. The world was far from ready yet to forget its prime VIP. Work still lay ahead of him in abundance: it was the therapy he needed and, to complete the cure, he had the companionship of yet another woman of outstanding merit.

Amalia Coutsouri-Voureka, a young Greek medical student, arrived at the Wright-Fleming Institute in 1946 to study under Fleming. Her 'passport' was a British Council Scholarship which she had won on the strength of outstanding academic potential and her service as a member of the Greek Resistance during the German occupation of her country. Refusal to recognize the overlordship of the Germans and the help she had given some of their victims earned Amalia Coutsouri-Voureka a period in jail in 1941.

Thirty years later, in 1971, after four years of active opposition to a military junta which had usurped power in Greece, she was to find herself again in prison and then deported.

Lady Amalia Fleming

When Fleming resumed his travels in 1950, he had a year of constant activity ahead of him. He made a fourth visit to the United States, toured Brazil, and visited the cities of Dublin, Milan, Rome and Brussels. At the University of Brussels, he delivered a speech in French prepared by Amalia Coutsouri-Voureka and painstakingly committed to memory by him. In December, he was in Stockholm for a meeting of the Nobel Institute.

A tour of Pakistan was all the globe-trotting Fleming did in 1951. For the first time in eight or nine years, he was able to spend most of his time at home. Amalia Coutsouri-Voureka, who had been taken on to the staff of the Wright-Fleming Institute by Fleming on completion of her Scholarship, and was now doing outstanding work as a bacteriologist, was invited to The Dhoon for the first time. There, she worked in the laboratory Fleming had set up for himself.

A later study of Fleming at work.

According to Amalia, she was often impressed by Fleming's ability to understand the meaning and cause of things. "If I had a problem which seemed difficult and confused to me," she said, "if I felt I was helplessly searching my way in a thick wood, he used to find the solution immediately. He gave me the impression that he was looking at this inscrutable forest from above, and that he could easily and clearly see the tortuous little path out, and where it led."

Fleming's courtship of Amalia Coutsouri-Voureka came to full flower in 1952. Much to his disappointment, Amalia had gone back to Athens to reorganize the bacteriological and haemotological laboratories in Evangelismos Hospital. Some correspondence passed between them and he sent her a portrait of himself by John Wheatley.

A meeting of the World Medical Association drew Fleming to Athens in October 1952. There to meet him was Amalia, charged by the University of Athens with looking after Fleming throughout his visit. Happy to be reunited with Amalia, Fleming revelled in the warmth of welcome he received from ordinary people wherever he went in her beloved country. Official engagements brought him lunch with the King and Queen, the Freedom of Athens, membership of the Academy of Athens, and a branch cut from the olive tree in whose shade, it is believed, Plato taught his pupils.

Ceremonial over, Amalia showed Fleming some of the hallowed parts of Greece – Corinth, 1000 years older than Christianity; the Temple of Aesculapius, the god of medicine; the theatre of Epidaurus; Argos, another of the ancient cities of Greece; Mycenae, centre of the great Easter-Mediterranean civilization; Olympia where the Olympic Games originated; Delphi, centre of the earth and seat of the Oracle of the Pythian Apollo.

With Amalia by his side, Fleming walked over ground bearing the footprints of the Gods.

Fleming was enchanted with Greece. Before leaving for home, the spell it had cast upon him charmed him into asking Amalia to marry him.

Fleming made what was to be his last visit to his native town of Darvel in 1952. On 27 June, he was principal guest at the J S School's annual closing ceremony in the Town Hall.

In addition to addressing the pupils of his old school, Sir Alexander presented the first Dux Medal to bear his name. The recipient was Frank Donnelly, now the Rector of Kilmarnock Academy.

The Dux Medal is of special interest. On the suggestion of Mr William Gray, manager of the local branch of the Clydesdale Bank, Sir Alexander agreed to give his name to the Medal. And, remembering that the French Mint had just struck a medal commemorating his discovery of penicillin, he suggested to Mr Gray and the J S School headmaster, Mr Alexander Clark, that they should ask the Mint to sell them copies.

The approach to the French Mint was successful. Mr Clark purchased 25 medals, and it was one of these, with the name of the winner engraved on the rim, that Sir Alexander handed over to Frank Donnelly.

Early in 1953, Fleming went off once more on his own, this time to tour India. Wherever he went, crowds greeted him with the kind of adulation he had already experienced in so many other countries. Soon after his return, on 9 April, Fleming and Amalia were married in Chelsea Registry Office. A week later, they left for Cuba and a fortnight of relaxation in the care of Margarita Tamargo, who had worked with them at the Wright-Fleming Institute.

Lady Amalia & Sir Alec in Rome, 1953.

From Cuba, the Flemings went to New York, Fleming's fifth visit to the United States. There they met old friends, and Sir Alexander got caught up as usual in a non-stop series of lectures and radio, TV and press interviews.

Returning home, the Flemings settled back into work at the Institute. During the week, they lived in the Danvers Street house and, at weekends, they retired to The Dhoon. Amalia's versatility came to the rescue when illness prevented Fleming from fulfilling a speaking appointment at "Les Journees Medicales" in Nice. At his request, she travelled to Nice and delivered the speech for him.

The following year, 1954, saw Amalia once again playing the role of stand-in for her husband on the occasion of a visit to Bordeaux University. Sir Alexander had prepared his speech in English but, before he could deliver it, the Dean, Professor Portmann, asked Amalia to translate it into French and deliver it for him. She obliged.

Fleming resigned as Principal of the Wright-Fleming Institute in January 1955, but, retaining his laboratory, he went on with his daily work as usual. A bout of 'flu laid him low in February, but he recovered and, come March, he was looking forward to visiting Greece, Turkey and the Lebanon with Amalia.

On Thursday 10 March, Fleming was given an anti-typhoid vaccination in preparation for his journey. The following morning, Friday 11 March, he had an attack of nausea and had to go back to bed. Amalia phoned Dr Hunt and left her husband so that she could go and dress. In her absence, Dr Hunt phoned and was told by Fleming not to worry about him but to attend to his other patients.

When Amalia returned, Fleming spoke of a pain in his chest. He died of a heart attack almost immediately.

Fleming's importance to Mankind no doubt persuaded the nation that he should lie with other illustrious dead in the Crypt of St Paul's Cathedral. And yet, one cannot but feel that Sir Alexander, had he been given a choice, would have chosen to lie under the vault of Heaven, somewhere in his native Ayrshire, and not under the vault of a cathedral 400 miles away. Fleming's body may be in London but his spirit surely and eternally inhabits the earthly presence that is Lochfield.

Fleming's body is carried into St Paul's. Lady Fleming and son, Robert, follow immediately behind.

The St Paul's service was attended by many of Fleming's relatives and personal friends, nursing and general staff of St Mary's, members of the medical profession, and colleagues from the Wright-Fleming Institute. Mr Randolph Churchill represented the Prime Minister.

Professor C A Pannett, a friend of Fleming since their earliest days at St Mary's, gave the eulogy. The Dean, The Very Rev.

W R Matthews, conducted the service and took as his text a passage from Ecclesiastes:

> "Honour a physician with the honour due unto him for the uses which ye may have for him: for the Lord hath created him. For of the Most High cometh healing, and he shall receive honour of the King. The skill of the physician shall lift up his head; and in the sight of great men he shall be in admiration. The Lord hath created medicines out of the earth; and he that is wise will not abhor them. Was not the water made sweet with wood, that the virtue thereof might be known? And He hath given men skill, that He might be honoured in His marvellous works. With such doth He heal men and taketh away their pains."

The week after the service in St Paul's, on Thursday 24 March, the staff of St Mary's took part in a private service of thanksgiving for the life of their colleague, Sir Alexander.

Lady Fleming continued to live on in London until 1962. Though her home had been where her husband was when he was alive, she felt her native land calling her back. The call was irresistible to her. Gradually, she transferred her belongings to Athens and, by March 1967, she had taken up residence in the Greek capital. Five weeks later, a military junta had taken over her country. Still passionately opposed to usurpers, Amalia Fleming actively opposed the junta, as she had done the Germans, and did what she could to help victims. In 1971, she was imprisoned, tried and forcibly deported to England, and there she remained until the restoration of democratic government in Greece in November 1974.

Lady Fleming is once more living in Athens. In "A Piece of Truth," published by Jonathan Cape, London, she writes of Greece under the Junta. Lady Fleming is now a member of the Greek Parliament, the European Parliament and sits on the Council of Europe.

Robert Fleming, Sir Alexander's son by his first wife, Sareen, is a doctor by profession with a general practice in Steeple Bumpstead, Sussex.

Fleming, the man of penicillin, was to be honoured as much in death as he had been in life. The flood of tributes continued locally, nationally and internationally.

This graphic portrait of Fleming illustrated Time Magazine's posthumous salute.

His native town of Darvel, which had already made him its first Freeman, added to the honour by laying out a garden in his memory, by marking his birthplace at Lochfield with a memorial stone and by creating an endowment for the purchase of prizes for pupils of Darvel School.

The Fleming Memorial Garden has occupied two sites Following a public meeting in Darvel on 19 January 1956, a memorial Fund Committee was formed under the chairmanship of the Provost, Mr Walter Fulton. This was the Committee which decided that a garden would be a suitable memorial; for this purpose, the sum of £4,740 was raised by public subscription.

Site of the original garden was on land to the south of Main Street just off the busy Ayrshire-Edinburgh road (A71) and facing the moorland hills protecting the farm of Lochfield where Sir Alexander was born. Alongside flowed the Glen Water whose upper reaches were the scene of many a childhood adventure for him.

The Fleming bust by E R Bevan in the Darvel memorial garden.

Ceremonial opening of the garden took place on Saturday, 23 April 1960. This duty, which included the unveiling of a bust of Sir Alexander by a close friend, the sculptor E R Bevan of London, was performed by Robert Cruickshank, Professor of Bacteriology at Edinburgh University.

Once a colleague of Fleming in the Research Laboratory at St Mary's Hospital, London, Professor Cruickshank showed how Fleming, the discoverer of penicillin, developed logically from Fleming, the son of a farmer.

"Fleming's boyhood at Lochfield," said Professor Cruickshank, "helped to develop his naturally-acute powers of observation. He was, above all, a biologist, interested in all natural phenomena and very knowledgeable about birds, flowers, and trees, as well as about bacteria. It was this observant eye that led to his two greatest discoveries - lysozyme and penicillin."

Professor Cruickshank continued: "Fleming appreciated beauty in many forms and took particular delight in flowers and gardens. It is fitting that Darvel should have chosen to perpetuate his memory in this lovely garden. It may become a shrine to which visitors from many lands will come and pay tribute to the discoverer of penicillin."

Lady Amalia Fleming, Sir Alexander's wife, was in the company which witnessed the ceremony on the banks of Glen Water. Accompanying her were Provost Fulton and members of Darvel Town Council, Darvel corporation officials, members of the Memorial Fund Committee, Professor Cruickshank, Dr Robert Fleming (Sir Alexander's son), Mr Robert Fleming (a brother), and Commander Geoffrey Hughes-Onslow, Convener of the County of Ayr.

Not long after the Memorial Garden was opened, damage from subsidence began to develop alarmingly. As a result, it was decided to move the garden to a safer location.

Hastings Square in the town centre was chosen. The garden became a 'piece de resistance' to the Square when its restoration was completed in the early 1960s.

Designed by Professor Wm J Smith, Royal College of Science and Technology, Glasgow, and laid out by Messrs G Reid & Son, Catrine, the original garden featured walls of hand-cut freestone, Yorkshire paving and teak seats.

Carvings of penicillin spores, magnified 18,000 times, decorated the base of two pillars. The central flower bed was circular and represented a petri dish used by bacteriologists in the cultivation of moulds.

"The flower beds will never be bare," says a report in the Irvine Valley News in April, 1960. "As flowers and shrubs spring up in their season, they will by symbotic of that new and continuing life which Sir Alexander's discovery of penicillin made possible for so many."

The granite stone marking Lochfield as Fleming's birthplace.

Besides meeting the cost of the garden, the Memorial Fund paid for the E R Bevan bust of Sir Alexander, the memorial stone of Cumberland granite which marks his birthplace at Lochfield, a portrait in oils by Grace Wheatley, and an endowment fund of £700 to provide "Fleming Memorial Prizes" at Darvel J S School.

The Lochfield Memorial Stone was sculpted by Messrs M Muir & Co Ltd, Kilmarnock, and was unveiled by Provost Walter Fulton, chairman of the Memorial Fund Committee, on Saturday 12 October, 1957.

Lady Amalia Fleming, wife of Sir Alexander, was in the company attending the ceremony. With her – Dr Robert Fleming, Sir Alexander's son, and Mr Robert Fleming, a brother of Sir Alexander.

Fleming's massive contribution as a research scientist inspired a move within the medical profession to create the Fleming Memorial Fund for Medical Research. The fund was set up in 1959 under the patronage of Her Majesty, The Queen Mother.

Launching the Fund, Lord Birkett, the president, said that Fleming had been rightly acclaimed as one of the great benefactors of the human race.

"The invaluable contribution of the research workers at Oxford," said Lord Birkett, "has resulted in penicillin being in daily use all over the world for the relief of suffering, the preservation of health, and the saving of human lives. It is, perhaps, not so widely known that Sir Alexander was not concerned to enrich himself by his discovery, but was content to devote himself unselfishly to the advancement of research and the conquest of disease. It is fitting, therefore, that this Memorial Fund should be instituted in his name."

In several countries of the world, memorials have been created in Fleming's memory. Streets and squares have been named after him. In London, the Ministry of Health building at Elephant and Castle is called Fleming House. A bust of

THE FLEMING MEMORIAL FUND FOR MEDICAL RESEARCH

Patron Her Majesty Queen Elizabeth The Queen Mother

Vice-Patrons The Earl of Halifax, KG, PC, OM, GCSI, GCMG, GCIE

Marshal of The Royal Air Force The Lord Tedder, GCB

President The Lord Birkett, PC

Chairman of Trustees The Lord Heyworth

Vice-Presidents (GREAT BRITAIN)

The Archbishop of Canterbury
The Lord Mayor of London
The Moderator of the General Assembly of the Church of Scotland
The Cardinal Archbishop of Westminster
The Moderator of the Free Church Federal Council
The Chief Rabbi
The Viscount Hailsham, PC, QC
The Rt. Hon. Hugh Gaitskell, CBE, MP
J. Grimond, Esq, MP
The President of the Royal Society
The Chairman of the Women's Voluntary Service
The Earl of Iveagh, KG, CB, CMG

Chairman of Executive Committee The Viscount Tenby, PC, TD, JP

Joint Honorary Treasurers Edgar E. Lawley, Esq.

Arthur H. Smith, Esq.

Fleming in Barcelona symbolizes the gratitude of the people of Spain.

Often the victim of fatal wounds in the bullring, Spain's matadors acknowledge their debt to penicillin with this bust of Fleming outside the bullring in Barcelona.

There are several portraits of Fleming. The Grace Wheatley portrait, which was part of Darvel's tribute, is now in the care of Kilmarnock and Loudoun District Council. Among the others is one by T C Dugdale which is kept in the Wright-Fleming Institute, another by Anna Zinkeisen which is in the boardroom of St Mary's Hospital, and a third by Ethel Gabain in the Imperial War Musem.

The Fleming bust in Barcelona is one of several. The Memorial Garden in Hastings Square, Darvel, features the one by E R Bevan. Another Bevan bust and one by E J Clark are in the Wright-Fleming Institue. There is a bronze by F Kovacs in Chelsea Town Hall, and yet another by E R Bevan in Witwatersrand University in South Africa.

Popular tribute in front of Fleming's bust in Barcelona.

MILESTO

— a chronological summar
years. (Reprinted by permissio

1928 'Penicillin' discovered by Fleming.

1941 "Acceptably pure" penicillin produced by Chain and Florey and used to treat nine cases of bacterial sepsis in man.

1944 Bulk quantities of penicillin manufactured by British, American and Canadian pharmaceutical industries for use on casualties from the second world war.

1957 The penicillin 'nucleus' — 6-aminopenicillanic acid — isloated in the Beecham Research Laboratories.

1959 The first semi-synthetic penicillin introduced — BROXIL* (phenethicillin).

1960 A penicillin active against penicillinase — producing staphylococci introduced — CELBENIN* (Methicillin).

1961 Introduction of the first broad-spectrum penicillin — PENBRITIN* (ampicillin).

ENICILLIN

r developments over 50
n Pharmaceuticals Ltd)

1963 The first of the isoxazolyl series of penicillins, orally active against penicillin-resistant staphylococci, became available as ORBENIN* (cloxacillin). Later developments in this area yielded FLOXAPEN* (flucloxacillin).

1967 The first penicillin active against pseudomonas became available as PYOPEN* (carbenicillin).

1972 Introduction of a new broad-spectrum anti-biotic effective for the treatment of a wide range of commonly occuring bacterial infections – AMOXIL* (amoxycillin).

1974 Introduction of an oral penicillin effective in the treatment of pseudomonal urinary tract infections – UTICILLIN* (carfecillin).

1975 The first penicillin pro-drug introduced, the broad-spectrum agent TALPEN* (talampicillin).

1979 An important new development in the treatment of life threatening infection – TICAR* (ticarcillin).

* Registered

Today, half a century and more since Alexander Fleming's discovery in 1928 that a penicillin mould could stop the growth of bacteria in the body, the pharmaceutical industry all over the world is producing massive quantities of penicillin, synthetically structured to combat many forms of infection.

The Control Room (Beecham).

By a happy chance, Beecham Pharmaceuticals, a part of the British Beecham Group, is manufacturing penicillin G in a factory in Irvine's modern industrial estate – no more than 20 miles from the farm of Lochfield where Fleming was born.

Beecham's interest in penicillin goes back more than twenty-five years. Originally manufacturers of well-known proprietary medicines, and other consumer products, they decided to devote a major part of their research resources to the development of penicillin. Beecham Research Laboratories had been formed some years earlier. A team of scientists was assembled and charged with the job of overcoming the deficiencies of penicillin G, the name given to the form of the drug which was being produced in Britain, Canada and the United States at the end of the 1939-45 war.

Some of the ancillary vessels which sterilize the raw materials before they are fed into production fermenters (Beecham).

Two years after beginning their work (1957), the Beecham scientists managed to isolate the penicillin nucleus. Appropriately enough, the breakthrough was made at Beecham's Brockham Park Research Laboratories, Surrey, an establishment which Fleming himself had opened ten years previously.

At the same time as they isolated the penicillin nucleus, the Beecham team found a method of attaching synthetic side-chains to the nucleus and so produced the first of the semi-synthetic penicillins so widely in use today.

Tanks containing raw materials (Beecham).

Production of the penicillin was concentrated by Beecham in a factory which they built at Worthing in 1959. Additional production capacity was soon required and the Beecham plant at Irvine was built at an original cost of £14,600,000. 600 people are employed on the production of penicillin G, the basic raw material for the firm's extensive range of antibiotics, and also the side chain for Amoxycillin, one of the most widely used broad spectrum semi-synthetic penicillins.

The penicillin G manufactured at Irvine goes to Beecham factories throughout the world for conversion into semi-synthetic penicillins.

The fermentation plant (Beecham).

General view of the Beecham plant on Irvine Industrial Estate.

FLEMING'S HONOURS

"By strangers honour'd, and by strangers mourned."

1902 Senior Open Entrance Scholarship in Natural Science, St Mary's Hospital Medical School.

1902-06 Almost all class prizes and scholarships at St Mary's Hospital Medical School.

1903 Medal, Swimming Club, London Scottish Regiment Volunteers.

1906 Licentiate Royal College of Physicians. Member Royal College of Surgeons, 26th July.

1906 Medal, Rifle Competition.

1908 M.B., B.S.(London). Gold Medal.

1908 Cheadle Gold Medal in Clinical Medicine, St Mary's Hospital.

1908 Medal, The Daily Telegraph Rifle Competition.

1909 Fellow of the Royal College of Surgeons of England, June.

1909 Territorial Force Efficiency Medal.

1914 Monthly Medal, West Middlesex Golf Club.

1919 Hunterian Professor, Royal College of Surgeons of England.

1919 Assistant Director of the Inoculation Department at St Mary's Hospital, 7th July.

1928 Professor of Bacteriology, London University, at St Mary's Hospital Medical School, 18th July.

1929 Arris and Gale Lecturer, Royal College of Surgeons.

1932 President of the Section of Pathology, Royal Society of Medicine.

1941 William Julius Mickle Fellowship, University of London.

1941 President of Comparative Medicine, Royal Society of Medicine.

1943 Fellow of the Royal Society, 11th March.

1943 Award of Distinction of American Pharmaceutical Manufacturers Association, 13th December.

1944 Foreign Associate of Royal Physiographic Society of Lund, Sweden, 8th March.

1944 Fellow of the Royal College of Physicians, 21st May.

1944 Knight Batchelor, 4th July.

1944 John Scott Medal and Prize – City Guild of Philadelphia, 21st July.

1944 Charles Mickle Fellowship, University of Toronto, 10th December.

1944 First Lister Memorial Lecturer, Society of Chemical Industry.

1944 Robert Campbell Orator (Medal). Ulster Medical Society.

1945 Honorary Freeman and Liveryman of the Dyers' Company of the City of London, 2nd May.

1945 Honorary Freeman of the Borough of Paddington, 17th May.

1945 Honorary D.Sc. University of Princeton, 13th June.

1945 Honorary D.Sc. University of Pennsylvania, 18th June.

1945 Honorary D.Sc. University of Harvard, 28th June.

1945 Honary Fellow Medical Chirurgical Society, Montreal, 19th July.

1945 Cameron Prize in Practical Therapeutics, University of Edinburgh, 11th July.

1945 Humanitarian Award,Variety Clubs of America, 25th July.

1945 Medaille d'honneur de service de Sante Militaire, France, 31st August.

1945 Commander of the Order of Public Health, France, 5th September.

1945 Louis Pasteur Medal (Institut Pasteur) 6th September.

1945 Commander of the Legion of Honour, France, 18th September.

1945 Doctor Honoris Causa of Medicine and Surgery, University of Rome, 18th September.

1945 Doctor Honoris Causa of Medicine, University of Brussels, 6th October.

1945 Nobel Laureate in Physiology and Medicine, 25th October.

1945 Honorary Member of the Philadelphia College of Pharmacy and Science, 5th November.

1945 Jydsk Medicinsk Selskab, Alresmeaiem, 18th November.

1945 Doctor Honoris Causa of Medicine, University of Louvain, 30th November.

1945 Doctor Honoris Causa, University of Paris, M.D. 15th December.

1945 Medal of Honour, Canadian Pharmaceutical Manufacturers.

1945 President of the Society for General Microbiology.

1945 Honorary D.Sc. University of Durham.

1945 Honorary Member, Royal Society of New Zealand.

1945 Doctor Honoris Causa of Medicine, University of Liege.

1945 Medal of the City of Liege.

1945 Moxon Medal, Royal College of Physicians.

1945 Corresponding Member of the Societe Nationale des Sciences naturelles et Mathematiques de Cherbourg.

1945 Honorary Member of Royal Medical Society, Edinburgh.

1945 Honorary Fellow of Jutland Medical Society.

1945 Cutter Lecturer, Harvard University.

1945 Associe Etranger, Academie de Medicine, Paris.

1945 Honorary Member of the Society of American Bacteriologists.

1945 Hebra. Dec. Fac. Med. Virdobonensis. Sir Alexander Fleming gratio amino.

1945 Honorary Award of the Schroeder Foundation.

1946 Correspondent Member of Academy of Sciences — Institute of France, 11th February.

1946 Member of Pontifical Academy of Sciences. 12th March.

1946 Honorary Professor, University of Brazil, 10th April.

1946 Fellow of the Eingelige Danski Videnskabernes Selskab (Royal Danish Academy of Sciences and Letters), 12th April.

1946 Honorary Member, Academia de Medicina, Buenos Aires, 6th June.

1946 Honorary Member of Pathological Section, Royal Society of Medicine, 2nd July.

1946 Honorary D. Sc. University of Dublin, 3rd July.

1946 Honorary M.D., University of Athens, 6th July.

1946 Honorary Doctor of Science, Queen's University, Belfast, 10th July,

1946 Honorary Member, College of Surgeons, Brazil, 5th September.

1946 Honorary Member of Academy of Medicine, Turin, 4th October.

1946 Freedom of Burgh of Darvel, 26th October.

1946	Gold Medal, Royal College of Surgeons of England, 14th November.
1946	Honorary Fellow of Institute of Medical Laboratory Technology.
1946	"Harben" Gold Medal, Royal Institue of Public Health and Hygiene.
1946	Knight of Mark Twain.
1946	Honorary Member of Philadelphia College of Pharmacy and Science.
1946	Honorary Fellow of Royal College of Physicians, Edinburgh.
1946	Medal in Therapeutics, Worshipful Society of Apothecaries. London.
1946	Albert Gold Medal. Royal Society of Arts.
1946	Foreign Honorary Member of Royal Academy of Medicine, Brussels
1946	Honorary President, Centre of Information and Study of Antibiotics, Milan.
1946	Honorary Member of Academy of Medicine, Brazil.
1946	Honorary Member, Medical Society of Lombardy.
1946	Honorary Member, Shut-Ins Association of America.
1947	Citation of the Order of the Purple Heart, U.S.A. 11th May.
1947	Honorary Fellow, Greek Surgical Society, 26th May.
1947	Gold Medal, Royal Society of Medicine, 17th June.
1947	Honorary LL.D., St Andrew's University, 4th September.
1947	Member Lynceorum Academia, Rome, 5th October.
1947	Medal for Merit, U.S.A. 13th October.
1947	Corresponding Member, Societe Philomathique, Paris.
1947	Honorary Member, the Wiener Gesellschaft der Aertze.
1947	Honorary Fellow, Royal Society of Edinburgh.
1947	Fellow of the Academie Septentrionale, France.
1948	Member of the Athenaeum, 19th January.
1948	Doctor Honoris Causa Medicine, Graz, 3rd May.
1948	Honorary D.Sc. University of London, 26th May.
1948	Honorary Member, Royal Academy of Medicine, Barcelona, 3rd June.
1948	President of Honor, Sociedad Medica de Hospitals, Sevilla, 5th June.
1948	Honorary Member, Sociedad Espanol de Higiene. 8th June.

1948 Honorary Member, Royal Academy of Medicine, Seville, 8th June.

1948 Honorary Member, Ateneo, Seville, 8th June.

1948 Grand Cross of Alphsonso (X), el Sabio, Spain, 11th June.

1948 Honorary D.Sc. Madrid, 12th June.

1948 Honorary Member, Royal Academy of Medicine, Madrid, 13th June.

1948 Professor Emeritus of Bacteriology in the University of London, 1st October.

1948 Gold Medal, Royal Academy of Medicine, Seville.

1948 Addingham Medal.

1949 Honorary Freeman of the Borough of Chelsea, 16th March.

1949 Honorary Member, Instituto Brasileiro de Historia da Medicina, 17th May.

1949 Actonian Prize, July.

1949 Freeman of the City of Verona, Italy, 28th July.

1949 Grand Cross of the Order of Phoenix, Greece, 16th September.

1949 Honorary D. Sc. Bristol University, 19th October.

1949 Honorary Life Membership 4-H Clubs, U.S.A.

1949 Honorary Member Future Farmers Association, U.S.A.

1949 Chief Doy-Gei-Taun (Maker of Great Medicine), Honorary Member Kiowa Tribe, U.S.A.

1949 "Grand Croix" Order of Chypre.

1949 Past Grand Warden, United Grand Lodge of England.

1949 Permanent Honorary Member of the Caledonian Club.

1949 Honorary Member. Savage Club.

1949 Honorary Member, Societa per lo Studio delle Malattie Infettive e Parasitarie, Italy.

1950 Honorary D. Sc. The National University of Ireland, 3rd July.

1950 Honorary Member, National Society for the Prevention of Blindness, 21st July.

1950 Gold Medal, American College of Chest Physicians.

1951 Member, Reale Accademia Internazionale del Parnaso, 16th February.

1951 Honorary Member of the Pakistan Medical Association, 8th April.

1951 Honorary Member, National Institute of Sciences of India.

1951 Sir Devaprasad Sarvadhikary Gold Medal(University of Calcutta).

1951 Lord Rector, University of Edinburgh.

1952 Cross of Officer of Merito Insigni. Belgian National Foundation of Charity, 12th May.

1952 Doctor Honoris Causa in Medicine, University of Salonika, 8th October.

1952 Honorary Member of the Greek Paediatricians Society, 10th October.

1952 Honorary Citizen of the City of Salonika, Greece, 16th Ocotober.

1952 Honorary President, Medical Society of Salonika, Greece, 22nd October.

1952 Gold Medal of Athens, 31st October.

1952 Foreign Member of the Academy of Athens, October.

1952 Honorary President of the Greek Society of Microbiology and Hygiene, 7th November.

1952 Honorary Citizen of Athens, 31st October.

1952 Honorary Member of almost all Medical Societies in Greece.

1952 Honorary Citizen of Kastoria.

1952 Honorary Member, Societe Francaise de Biologie Medicale.

1952 Foreign Member, Royal Netherlands Academy of Sciences and Letters.

1953 Honorary Member, Societas Medica Havniensis, 5th February.

1953 Honorary Member, Cuban Society of Clinical Pathology (Laboratorios Clinicos) 10th April.

1953 Honorary Member, Royal Society of British Sculptors, 16th April.

1953 Honorary Member, Cuban Good Neighbour Foundation, 20th April.

1953 Honorary Member, National Pharmaceutical College of Cuba, 21st April.

1953 Honorary Member de la Assoc. de Estudiantes de Med., University La Habana, 23rd April.

1953 Grand Cross, Orden de Honor y Merito of Cuban Red Cross, 23rd April.

1953 Grand Commander, Order of Carlos Finlay, 23rd April.

1953 Honorary Professor of the University of Habana, 28th April.

1953 Honorary Member, Colegio Medico Nacional de Cuba, 28th April.

1953	Honorary Member, National College of Pharmacists, Cuba.
1953	Grand Lodge Medal for Distinguished Achievement, (Grand Lodge of Free and Accepted Masons of the State of New Jersey) 5th May.
1953	Honorary Member, Academia de Letras Jose de Alencar, Brazil, 7th June.
1953	Honorary Member, Botanical Society of Cuba, 29th September.
1953	Honorary Member, Brazilian Association of Ex-Combatants, 24th October.
1953	Doctor Honoris Causa in Law, University of Edinburgh, November
1953	Honorary Member, Copenhagen Medical Society.
1953	Honorary Citizen of Mikonos, Greece.
1954	Foreign Associate, l'Academie des sciences de l'Institut de France, 15th February.
1954	D.Sc. University of Utah, 27th March.
1954	Honorary Member, American Academy of General Practice, March
1954	Commissioned Kentucky Colonel, 7th April.
1954	Award for Merit, University of Louisville, 13th April.
1954	Honorary Member, Medical Society Ribeirao Preto, 4th May.
1954	Honorary Member, Academy of Medicine, Sao Paulo, 10th May.
1954	Citizen of City of Sao Paulo, 11th May.
1954	Ordem Do Estilingue (Order of the Catapult), Ribeirao Preto, 11th May.
1954	Citizen of Ribeirao Preto, 11th May.
1954	Honorary Member of Centro Academico XXV de Janeiro, 13th May.
1954	Doctor Honoris Causa, University of Sao Paulo, 13th May.
1954	Honorary Member, Medical Association of Santos, 14th May.
1954	Honorary Member, Escuela Paulista Medicina, May.
1954	Honorary Fellow, Royal Society of Medicine, 20th July.
1954	Citizen of State of Sao Paulo.
1954	Honorary Member, Academy of Pharmacology and Odontology, Sao Paulo.
1954	Honorary Member, Central Academy Pereira Barretto.

1954	Citation from University of Sao Paulo.
1954	Citizen of Honour, Town of Bordeaux, 15th November.
1954	Doctor Honoris Causa, University of Bordeaux, 15th November.
1954	Freeman of the Company of Barbers of London, 7th December.
1954	Vice-President Emeritus of the Royal Sanitary Institute.
1954	Commander of "Compagnons du Bontemps Medoc."
1954	Jurade du St. Emilion.
1954	Honorary Member of the Alpha Omega Alpha of the University of Oklahoma.
1954	Honorary Member of the Brazilian Association of Ex-Combatants.
1954	Diploma, Federation Internationale des Arts des Lettres et des Sciences.
1955	Doctor Honoris Causa Veterinary Medicine, University of Vienna, 10th March.

SIR ALEXANDER FLEMING

Calm, unperturbed, and difficult to sway,
Upon each problem steadily intent,
His mind and fingers by their interplay
Achieved solution by experiment.
In ceaseless toil the years came and went
Till came that day
he seized the millionth chance
Gained for himself a lasting monument
And for his art unparalleled advance.
He was a modest man, and, spite of fame,
And all the world's
most fulsome adulation
Remained unspoilt and evermore the same
Without a trace of pride or affectation.
As he began, so was he to the end;
It is an honour to have been his friend.

Zachary Cope

FLEMING'S PHILOSOPHY

(Culled from his public addresses)

"It seems rather a pity that some politicians are not disciples of Robert Burns. Some of them have had worldly (and wordy) success, some have amassed fortunes . . . . but Burns lives on and they will be forgotten."

"What is success? It might be defined as achievement of one's ambition. If we accept this simple definition, then everyone is in some way successful and no one is completely successful."

"Robert Burns has been the man who, perhaps more than any other, has helped to bind Scotsmen together. His Immortal Memory is proclaimed on his birthday in January in all parts of the world, not in serious debate, but in pleasant company with food and drink in surroundings where disputes can easily be settled."

"The constitution of the U.S.A. has it that all men are created equal. This cannot be true. Apart from anything else, we have the whole science of genetics to show that there must be enormous differences between individuals."

"Many men have gained success at the expense of others. Fortunately, in my profession, medicine, success does not readily come by harming other people. What leads to success is pure gain to the community."

"Many people work hard and sometimes think. Many just work hard and I am afraid many do not even do that."

"It may be said that I have achieved success. I suppose I have. But, in my success, as in the success of many others, fate or destiny, fortune or chance, call it what you will, has had a good deal to do with it."

"The rich man's son has often been at a disadvantage in that he had not the incentive of need to spur him on. The son of the poor man had too much need and had to earn his living at an early age. But this is really a weeding out process, for, whether rich or poor, the youth with the will to work can learn the things outside his daily task and often find his true bent."

"As the world becomes more complicated, so we are less able to carry through anything to a successful conclusion without the collaboration of others."

"In medicine, we do not have national boundaries. Our research work is published, and it is free for all the world to read and use. In the perfect world, this free inter-change of knowledge would be general. But, we see every day that this world is far from perfect."

"To be humble (in the Army – Ed) was a great advantage. There was no need for you to think, you just did as you were told. The officers, on the other hand, had to do a lot of hard thinking, since, as often as not, they did not know what ought to be done. But they had to do something, or pass the buck to the Colour Sergeant."

"Some people think that medical students should spend all their time learning medicine and should give up games. I don't agree. There is far more in medicine than mere book-work. You have to know men and you have to know human nature. There is no better way to learn about human nature than indulging in sports."

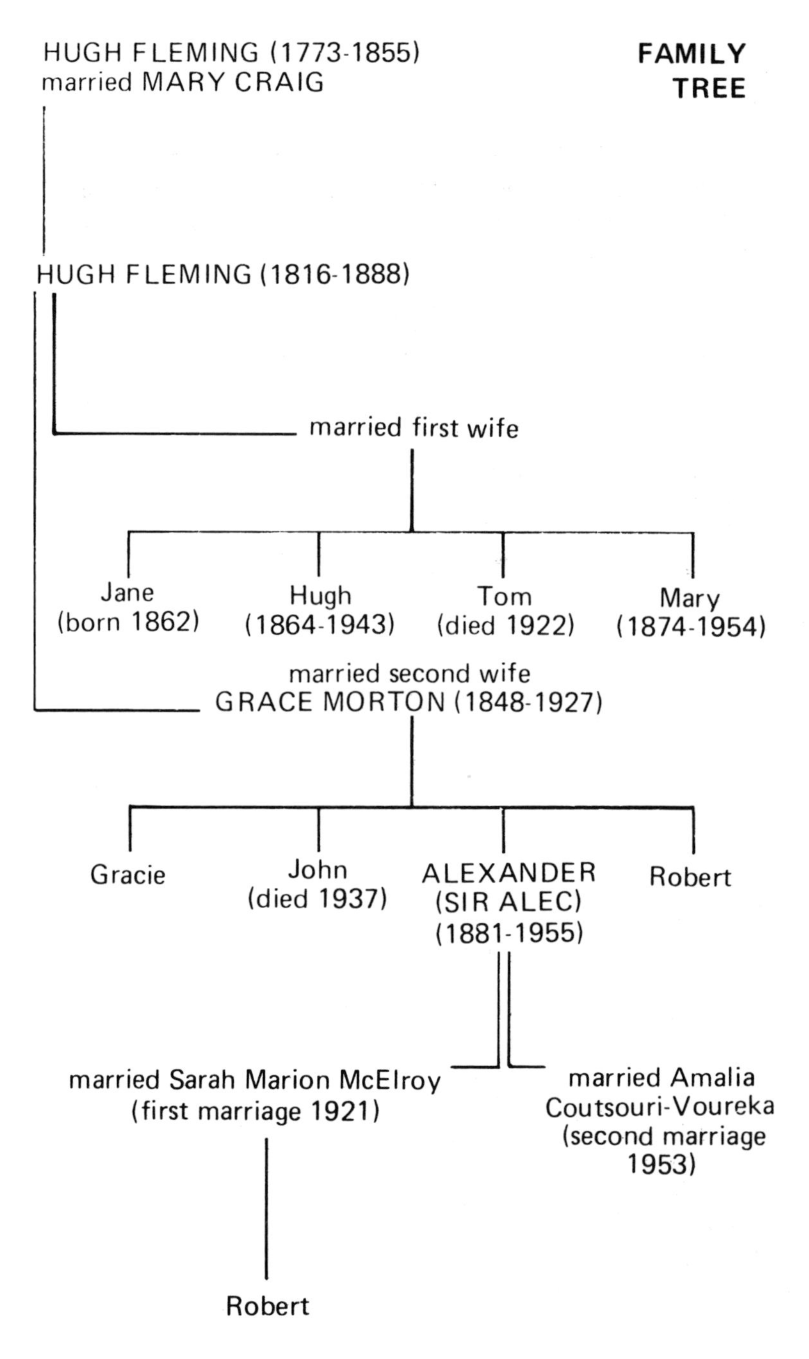
HUGH FLEMING (1773-1855)
married MARY CRAIG
FAMILY TREE
HUGH FLEMING (1816-1888)
married first wife
Jane (born 1862)
Hugh (1864-1943)
Tom (died 1922)
Mary (1874-1954)
married second wife
GRACE MORTON (1848-1927)
Gracie
John (died 1937)
ALEXANDER (SIR ALEC) (1881-1955)
Robert
married Sarah Marion McElroy (first marriage 1921)
married Amalia Coutsouri-Voureka (second marriage 1953)
Robert

ACKNOWLEDGEMENTS

The author wishes to express his indebtedness to the following sources of reference

"The Life of Sir Alexander Fleming" André Maurois

"Sir Alexander Fleming" Robert Fleming

"Lysozyme" Lady Amalia Fleming

"A Piece of Truth" Lady Amalia Fleming

Keesing's Contemporary Archives

"History of St Mary's Hospital Medical School" Zachary Cope

Dictionary of National Biography

"Book of Old Darvel" Alex S McLeod

Beecham Group Ltd., Brentford, Middlesex

Dr Robert Fleming, Steeple Bumpstead, Sussex

Dr G R Butler, St Andrew's University

Files of Kilmarnock Standard

Files of Irvine Valley News

Records of Darvel Town Council

Records of Kilmarnock & Loudoun District Council

Staff of Dick Institute, Kilmarnock

Mr William Gray, Symington, Kilmarnock

Miss Margaret Young, Darvel

Mr George Young, Darvel

Mr Alexander Clark, Kilmarnock

Mr James McCulloch, Bishopbriggs